DEATH CEREMONY

THE JOURNEY FROM BIRTH TO DEATH

THRINADH SAI

ISBN 979-888591437-6

To my Mother

Contents

"Death is the most terrible of all things, for it is the end, and nothing is thought to be either good or bad for the dead."

- Aristotle

"One has to pay dearly for immortality; one has to die several times while one is still alive."

-FRIEDRICH NIETZSCHE

Acknowledgements

I want to thank my family and friends for always being there for me. I must thank Kalpa, Ankita, Mohan, Naidu for inspiring me to write this book; without you all, it would not have been possible.

Preface

Death is a ubiquitous and unavoidable phenomenon in the human experience that cannot be avoided or postponed. Death is one of the few concepts that span cultural boundaries, is gender and ethnically agnostic, and is therefore much beyond our ability to manage. Death is definite in the sense that it will happen to everyone, but it is unknown in terms of when or how it will happen. Death is defined biologically as the termination of working organs and can be detected by physiological indications such as heart rate, blood pressure, endocrine hormone levels, or brain function.

The physical indications of death and their occurrence are researched in terms of human behavior and cognition leading up to and following one's own death or the death of another in the subject of psychology. Death and mortality are philosophically contested and explained in a variety of ways.

Plato, for example, maintains that the soul is immortal and will continue to exist (in a spiritual sense) even after the physical annihilation of the body. He adds that people's dread of death is understandable, but death should be considered as the culmination of life. Epicurus, on the other hand, says that the soul is mortal and dies when the body dies since the two exist in one. He says that people are irrational in their fear of death since, once death happens, the experience is gone and the person is unable to identify the anguish of the experience.

The notion that death instills dread is unquestionably correct. This normal human fear of death serves as the foundation for death-related psychological studies.

Psychology studies human reactions to death rather than the actual experience of death. Psychologists investigate death via ideas that aim to explain our behaviors leading up to our own deaths and following the deaths of others in order to better comprehend this caused worry and terror.

This includes mortality salience, which refers to a person's recognition that death is unavoidable. This awareness of being helpless to avoid death causes cognitive dissonance since humans have an inherent wish to live; this is known as the fear management theory. These principles enable psychologists to comprehend the thoughts, feelings, and behaviors that occur when people contemplate death. There are various characteristics of death that might influence people's perceptions and reactions to it. Age, just world views, the worth of human life, belief in an afterlife, readiness, and the tragedy of death are all factors.

CHAPTER ONE

Live to Die

"We are not sure that we will even live tomorrow."

This truth is something you should keep in mind every day. For example, there's the Bollywood actor who died from an overdose due to heroin use; another person lost their life when they were run over by a car while wearing no seatbelt or doing other dangerous things without paying attention. When you are told that a friend or loved one has died, it's impossible not to feel emotional. You remember the time when they woke up from their sleep and went about life as if nothing happened; there is no warning sign for death in our world today so this conversation makes senseless than ever before but also reminds us all too well - each event should be celebrated because we never know what tomorrow may bring!

There is something about the thought of death that makes you think more deeply about life and what it means to live. When someone dies, they often teach us some valuable lesson in their exit from this world- whether by teaching kindness or showing mercy towards others who are living while still serving a purpose for themselves within its society; there can't really be any wrong answer when considering why humans choose suicide (or at least try).

The thing I learned most clearly during my time working with those suffering through depression was just how important everyday moments could become if taken away - either literally Colorful Intelligence.

We all die. It's a fact of life that cannot be avoided, and the question everyone has on their mind - what happens after you pass away? Do your memories live on in another form or do they just disappear with time; does this mean there will never ever come any answers for us as humans about how we can find peace & meaning when something so fundamental seems unanswered at best (if not blindly doubted)? This may sound like rejection since most people don't know exactly where these feelings came from yet but I'd argue against themselves despite having an idea behind why things happened thus far during one's journey through existence.

When you are young, it is hard to think about the future. You don't know what your life will be like or when death may come for yourself- but as we grow older everything changes and now that time seems more precious than ever before because each day could potentially be our last on earth. There are many people who believe that tomorrow will always be. But the reality is, no one knows when their last day on earth shall come about; so it's best to enjoy what time you have with family and friends while making sure they remember how important these moments together really were!

When facing death, many people deny their illness. They do this to avoid the pain of losing someone or something that is precious for them - even if it means prolonging what could be a short life span in order to feel more time with those left behind and appreciated through memories made throughout your days together; there isn't always an answer as simple as "acceptance" when you're struggling between two worlds like we all are at some point during our journey here. I'm not going to let anything happen to me!

When the victim of trauma feels that their needs are not being met, they enter into an angry stage. They may ask "Why not?" or feel resentment towards others who have been healthy throughout this process and are now able to provide assistance for those in need because it's just not fair!

The person goes through two different types of stages during which emotions such as anger arise: first there's Relief And Planning - when everything seems possible again even though no solution has been found yet; then follows Grief When All Hope Is Lost. The bargaining process is a delicate balance of time and value. The person wants more than what they're given, but often can't find the worth in their life without it being granted by someone else--in this case, God or fate itself would be responsible for giving them something better if only He were able at such late hours when everyone has already asleep (and hopefully content).

The certainty of death leads to depression, isolation, and hopelessness as people face their final days. It's often said that we don't really know how much time someone has left until they're told it by an equally uncertain illness or tragedy, but this logic doesn't seem applicable in some cases because when you have a terminal condition like cancer there isn't always exactly one clear moment where everything changes – though certainly, some events may trigger feelings ranging from fear all the way up towards acceptance.

The final stage of the regret process is acceptance. A person in a life-threatening condition accepts that he or she will die, and prepares for their future as death approaches them withdrawing from their interest in problems outside this world until it's time to say goodbye lastly if they don't have enough resolve then maybe making sure all debts are paid off before passing away

This passage discusses how certain people go through different emotions when faced with an important event such as dying; one common feeling among those who realize what awaits at end times includes resignation (or even relief). They can also share their wishes for funeral arrangements and burial. It is almost void of feeling like the pain has gone away or something terrible happened that changed everything but you don't want to talk about it because now this everything feels final-the end before your long journey begins

The person should be able to communicate what they desire in regards towards how he/she wants things done during his lifetime through sharing thoughts on topics such as funeral site preparation & cremation urns, etc. while avoiding dwelling too heavily on emotional subjects which could make others uncomfortable.

To some, death is a forbidden subject that should not even be discussed. They refuse to think about their own deaths and instead focus on living life as if there would always be another day left in which they can enjoy all the things this world has to offer them

The thought of dying appalls many people because it feels like an admission defeat; after all, we're only alive today due largely thanks, so why admit failure now?

However, for some people dying is a very difficult topic to discuss or even think about. They refuse and struggle with questions on how they will die in the future because it's too painful

This passage talks about because death was once considered as something that shouldn't be talked about; however, now we realize this can make things worse when someone has passed away.

The day I die will be the most memorable of my life. It's not that it won't feel like any other yesterday or tomorrow, but there are so many things happening all at once- partings with loved ones being one of them; realizing how much time has passed since childhood memories came about in an instant because you're now facing your final moments on earth... When this happens to someone who doesn't know their eternal destination (as is often the case for poor people), then work loses its meaning. The person wants them to spend more time enjoying their life. I am not true enough for myself and so he had to compromise my feelings with an otherwise great place in this world

The man didn't express himself properly, which caused trouble when it came down from expressing what was really on his mind- leading him into making bad decisions about how much involvement there should be between us."

We all want to be in touch with our friends and loved ones when death is near, but many of us can't say goodbye because they lose contact. I myself wanted happiness- so instead of losing my ex-friends on Facebook or Twitter for example (which would make sense), I decided that it was best if we just stayed away from each other altogether!

I'm sure there must have been some reason why this happened; maybe something came up between both parties which caused them not able to communicate anymore? Whatever the case may be been: If only one side makes efforts towards contacting another then everything should fall into place again eventually.

We all have the power to make our own happiness. Many people are afraid of change and will stay in their comfort zones, but that's a decision they can make on behalf of themselves because there is no wrong or right way when it comes down to personal choice in this area

The idea behind being happy goes much deeper than just doing things for their own sake; instead, you should put yourself first by taking actions that increase your joyfulness levels--even if only slightly so! For some folks, these may include going outside once during a rainy day rather than watching TV inside where everything feels snugly dry as toast...or taking up jogging long distances rather

We all have a certain amount of time left. When that number is called, what will you leave behind? Will your last wish be for those around to remember how much they loved and cared about or could their memories simply fade with each passing day without ever being tested by any pain whatsoever because life isn't really like this sometimes...weeping over someone no longer living seems silly when there's so little awareness left inside ourselves as if everything has been taken from us already even though some things might still remain hidden away somewhere deep down inside where darkness resides alongside light at turns.

While the death of a person is always hard, it can be especially difficult when they are not only loved but also good friends. Grief often leads people through an initial phase where rejection and disbelief become main feelings before acceptance sets in eventually giving way to healing again over time- though many will never get over their sadness entirely which might make them persistently sad for years after losing someone close like this happened with family members or lovers; however there's hope!

It is hard to think about death, but it will happen. Usually when you realize that someone close has died their life becomes more clear and less confusing in your mind because all the pieces fit together now without any room for uncertainty or confusion about what happened

The person was gone from this world forever so there wasn't much left behind other than memories- which may be difficult at first given how sudden everything can feel after losing somebody dear (especially if they were really impacting), then again maybe not since many people find comfort(and closure)in doing things right by placing coffins inside funerals, etc.

When the body is buried, it becomes impossible for people to visit their loved ones and see how they've aged. All that remains are bones in an open field with nothing else around them - just coldness striking down on heartless ground Zero dignity or respect is given when someone's life ends like this; there should at least be some kind words spoken by relatives before moving on anything else so long after death has taken place.

Near-death experiences are reported to be more common than one would think. People who have experienced short deaths say that they were conscious at the time of their temporary exit from this world, but there's no way for us to verify if it really happened or not because most near-death patients don't remember anything about what happens before their brush with eternity.

What happens to a person when they die? The trappings of wealth, power, and status become irrelevant. Their assets such as cars or homes will be given away while work is either forgotten about completely by those who survived them in some cases it may even get redistributed among other people depending on how much time has passed since that individual's passing

The loved ones left behind go through many changes after losing someone so important but one thing remains consistent- life goes on because there must always continue moving forward despite our sorrows.

They go through a series of emotions as they start to understand that their love is gone. All the while, photos, and videos remind them how much someone else loved this person who now doesn't exist in any form except for what can be seen at certain cemeteries across America- plots where two people lay side by side forevermore waiting until somebody finds themselves again.

What happens to the human soul or spirit after death? This question has been pondered over for centuries and there are many answers. If you're Buddhist, like my mom—she doesn't believe in a Spirit any more than she believes in heaven; but if it's Christian then perhaps eternal life with God awaits them at their final destination depending on how good they were while living this life out here on earth... Whether one was raised by parents who taught him/her about Taoism (the Asian philosophical tradition), Buddhism conceived through Indian thought processes which see no pointes without suffering so as long. We all die. We don't know what happens to the soul after death, but there are some interesting beliefs out in this world that try to explain it - from religion and New Age philosophy alike!

Leading a healthy lifestyle is important because it teaches you to appreciate the life that God gave. If death were something we could avoid by not living in moderation, then people would never learn how precious their lives really are- which means they may end up taking unnecessary risks or giving up on making positive changes for themselves altogether! We should not live carelessly, such as jumping out of a plane with a parachute. Climbing mountains is also very dangerous and can lead to death if you don't take precautions for your health.

If we valued life enough then this would be something that crosses our minds before doing any sort of extreme sports or taking advantage when there are opportunities like illness strikes friends.

Life is all about living in the moment and not worrying too much. You might die tomorrow or five years from now but until then, what's wrong with taking it easy? It can be difficult to let go of our plans for after we're gone because who wants something boring like reality when there were so many possibilities ahead-like being an international cheerleader for instance!

I think one thing everyone should do while they still have their physical body intact (and preferably on earth), would involve exploring themselves as fully possible: study medicines/ therapies copiously.

What a beautiful sunset it was! I remember the first time that I watched one. You never forget your first kiss or who taught you how to ride a bike- they are always special moments in life which teach us all different lessons about what really matters, but especially death because as cliche as this may sound; when we're gone - done living -- there's nothing left behind except those simple pleasures: watching sunsets (or stars), playing games with friends/ family like crepe tickets versus Switzerland cheese maps; enjoying romantic relationships even though sometimes these things don't work out.

The beauty of life is that there are so many possibilities, but death provides us with an opportunity to really think about what matters. Learning how best to spend your time and energy can help you make the most out of any situation in which you find yourself without worrying if it will be worth remembering or not by memory later on down the road

A lot of people believe they need material things like nice homes and fancy cars when actually happiness comes from more simple pleasures such as good sex...traveling around etcetera. It's important though because sometimes these distractions cause problems within our personal relationships; this might lead them away from those who truly care about making. The best things in life are free. But there's a catch - they come with strings attached! For example, family and friends are great if you want to be loved unconditionally by someone who cares about your well-being deeply but knows how difficult it is sometimes for us as humans beings to close ourselves off from others out of fear or anxiety; leisure instruments can provide some much-needed solace when times seem tough because playing music helps calm our minds while also releasing endorphins which give rise positive feelings throughout the body (and helps make any task easier). These benefits might sound small compared to other potential outcomes on the area(s)of health.

Wisdom teaches us to live wisely in the present moment. Mindfulness means being aware of our senses - what we see, hear, and feel now while alive; it's not getting lost thoughtlessly on a sea of memories or future plans for tomorrow that may never come true." Wishing for a better future can make us forget about the importance of living in this very moment. We will only regret not being able to experience what we never had when it's too late, so why waste time? By following wise advice and making good decisions now you are assured that your worries over potential problems or regrets from missed opportunities won't plague your mind anymore

- because there isn't any room left!

We all know how it feels when we're sitting on the couch watching TV and our child starts asking us questions about life, like "What does this word mean?" or "Why are some people rich while others aren't?" And even though you might not be able to answer their queries with complete clarity right now because of work deadlines taking over your day-to-day living space; what if those things happened tomorrow morning after a long night's sleep where every single second counted--where everything turned out just fine in spite its problems. Would that make today seem less valuable then? Of course not!

The happiness myths are just that, but with a little bit of mindfulness and an eye on your blessings, you can find true joy in life. For example, one's health is absolutely key to enjoying the things it allows us time for!

I've seen so many people who have never had good quality of life because they were too busy worrying or fussing over other issues outside their control like money coming into savings accounts (which isn't really possible).

What do you want to be remembered as? Most people seem intent on being seen as a "well-off" person. They hope that their loved ones and colleagues will have good things to say about them, even if it's just for one thing they did in life! This is what our society considers great: money can't buy happiness but at least then we won't feel too bad when someone else has all the luck with wealth because everyone deserves some kind of treatment anyway – right?!

A few others would rather not leave any trace behind; instead choosing an anonymously private farewell where no-one knows who was really living beneath these words before reading. Death is the ultimate equalizer. It doesn't matter who you were before, after death all of our past lives comeuppance us in one way or another- whether it be wealth that was once power gone forever due to political turmoil; status symbols whose value has been lost with time because people no longer remember how they made their fortunes, etc... The lesson here isn't just about leaving behind something beautiful but also being generous enough so others can learn from your example too!

When someone dies, I feel sad and think about their death. Did they suffer in the afterlife? Is it quiet there for them now that they're gone? What does this mean to me as well- is their life after dead coming back around again or something similar where we'll all just continue living our lives without knowing if anything will change because of us being done talking altogether...afraid of dying with no answers forthcoming from whatever may come next; unable even hope. I like to think about the absurdity of life and how we were born for a short time.

There is something so capitalists about this idea - there must be some money worth dying over!

Western society is obsessed with working and achieving success. We neglect to take time for ourselves, let alone think about death which will come sooner than we realize if only because our lives are so fleeting in contrast to the enormity of existence itself

We should all start appreciating each moment as it comes rather than living through every day expecting something wonderful but never finding it while simultaneously denying ourselves any sense whatsoever towards happiness or fulfillment! We all want to live our lives meaningfully, but it isn't always possible. If someone believes that they are going to die someday then what would be their priority? Some people seek not only material goods and comforts necessary for comfortable life-also excess from those who worship wealth or power; each of these can never last forever so why do anything in this world as if you expect them will stop anytime soon!?

When I realized that death is a part of life, and getting older will never change the fact. This has changed my views on what it means to live well in this world with our minds-how we should treasure every moment because they could be gone tomorrow

Awareness from studying Buddhism about how short our lives really are made me think more deeply than before why people put so much effort into having fulfilling careers or loving partners etc., when there's no guarantee any single one thing can bring joy forever...and finally got an answer: It isn't just shoes; They're also insurance policies against disappointment! By focusing on the present moment, I endeavor to live wisely and give my life meaning. When it comes down to time or energy for something that could potentially be beneficial but isn't necessary just yet - like an activity in which you're already invested-I try not to let anything stop me! it seems as though nothing can stop me from doing what feels right for once - even if it's risky or not supported by society at large (or any given institution).

This new perspective on how valuable each moment truly is should be respected by everyone who seeks change because these decisions won't just affect you; they'll impact generations after yours too.

Now I think about it, especially when I learn of someone's death. Every day, I thank God for my many blessings, especially my good health. While expressing my creativity, good health, friendship, spirituality, and so on, I also focus on the vital ones. I'll try not to squander any time.

I'm not sure if there is an afterlife. I hope so, but I'm not sure. One of the most enigmatic questions I can address in this life is about life beyond death. Furthermore, when I die, I will be unable to answer this question, especially if death results in loss of consciousness, emptiness, and existence.

CHAPTER TWO

The tangle of hope

Our lives are filled with a lot of grief and misery. Some people are more affected by these dismal aspects of the human condition than others. However, with optimism, problems can be conquered. When your boss brings you into his office and sits you down on Friday evenings after you've worked long hours on a project, Hope offers us the strength to face the sufferings and frustrations brought by misfortune, perhaps unexpected job loss. "You have been expelled."

It was most likely an unexpected conclusion to the marriage. When you want to be loved, your wife is crying in bed. "I can't live with you anymore," she whispered as she turned to face you.

Probably an unanticipated car accident: A man in a hurry, texting on his smartphone, smashed his delivery trunk into your new blue Mustang, which you had saved for five years, and now tow trucked it to the scrap yard.

Despite the fact that we do not know how, when, where, or why our life narrative will finish, hope inspires us to endure, to press forward, into the darkness, despite life's hurdles.

Hope, according to psychologists, consists of three components: belief, purpose, and journey. A person who is optimistic believes that he will succeed. Second, the individual has a clear target direction or destination in mind. Third, the individual is aware of the method or methods by which he or she will achieve the desired result. So, hope is an attitude, a will, and a desire to believe that you will transcend. Hope also provides you with a road plan for achieving the desired result.

"Hope begins in the dark, obstinate hope, and the morning comes if you look if you attempt to do the right thing."

"Try again," hope always says to the mentality.

Consider for a moment that you have been transported into Earl's karmic-driven world. Most significantly, you'll feel helpless and depressed. Your mind descends into despair, and you consider suicide. When a love affair ends, you believe there will be no one for you in the future. If you lose your job, you may fear you will never be able to find another. When you are sick, you may believe that you may never heal. If you have a fatal illness, you persuade yourself that when you die, there will be no nothingness, no existence. You are experiencing existential angst.

What are the advantages of hope? Hope is the antidote to all forms of adversity and sorrow. Hope enables us to cope with traumatic circumstances such as an elderly parent dying in a hospital bed. When our lives are filled with tough conditions or tragic experiences, hope encourages us to endure. The notion of a new job to pay bills and buy money to fill some of life's comforts, such as a television, an iPad, a new pair of blue jeans, and a refrigerator with food, motivated the unemployed to look for work.

Hope aids a sick person's recovery and inspires them to do everything in their power to heal. "You will recover," it assures them.

Hope comforts the dying and provides them the strength to confront the unknown. It murmurs, "There is life after death." It provides solace to individuals who are grieving the loss of a loved one and allows them to progress through the five stages of grief, eventually accepting but never forgetting.

Faith is given as a gift by hope. It arouses a person's desire to believe, drives them to read the scriptures, participate in prayer and meditation, ponder the mysteries of life, and seek answers. Hope inspires us to live moral lives, to be empathetic and loving.

Hope is a spiritual practice that provides us with a "spiritual" sensation that allows us to feel awe, wonder, and joy. We may transcend nature, notice its beauty, live in peace, respect others, live intelligently, and trust in the unknown, the incompetent if we have hope. In difficult times, hope is an essential component of optimism, which teaches us to "live on the best opportunities." As a spiritual aid for helplessness, existentialism, and nihilism, hope is a medication.

Positive psychologists who have researched the science of happiness believe that hope is the signature strength, peace of mind, satisfaction, and life satisfaction that improves our well-being.

Life, for some, is a tomb of hope. Others define opportunities as those that encourage a person to attain the desired objective, overcome adversity, keep trying, and face the modest odds of success. What do those who are hopeful have in common?

To begin, a hopeful person feels that life will work out, that they will solve the problem, conquer disease, or recover from depression or bereavement. How did this optimistic mindset emerge? To begin, a hopeful individual engages in positive "self-talk." When confronted with a stressful scenario or adversity when negative thoughts enter one's mind, the optimistic person will tell themselves, "It works. I will find a method to conquer and succeed.

Second, even in the face of adversity, the optimistic individual envisions a positive outcome. For example, when a person becomes ill, he believes he is safe again. When not working, the employee is anticipated to be employed again by the company. When a person is alone, he or she fantasizes about finding a soul mate.

Third, when the situation is poisonous, such as when a person is terminally ill, the dying person focuses on the positive parts of the dreadful condition. The individual accepts his fate yet chooses to focus on the positive aspects of his or her life. A dying person, for example, may prioritize living in the present now, streamlining their affairs, spending time with loved ones, and achieving goals.

Fourth, a hopeful person lives in the present. Instead of fretting about the future, the individual concentrates on what today can do to make tomorrow a reality. A lonely person sitting alone at home on Friday, for example, can combat their loneliness and irritation by going to a singles dance or chatting with other lonely people on an online dating service.

Finally, hopeful people are endowed with the spirit of a specific faith. The spiritual person may be an agnostic who is not affiliated with any religion but believes in God and the afterlife. The spiritual person can benefit from all of the sages' spiritual knowledge. The spiritual person can believe in Buddhism's philosophy, which includes the concept of reincarnation. A person of faith, on the other hand, is a Christian who goes to church, studies the Bible, and prays for hope. Each of these people is self-assured, which is reassuring. It is the will to believe that answers their questions and overcomes their doubts, motivating them to hope for light when their lives are dark.

Hope is not a wishful concept or a magical thought. Hope is an emotion, a mentality, a belief, and inspiration that, despite failures and barriers, challenges and disasters, and the unknown final chapter in your life story, you believe that your life will function when you die. Breathe, there is another universe beyond this one.

When you have enough hope, you can do extraordinary feats. Christopher Reeves, a former American actor who was paralyzed after being thrown from his horse, became quadriplegic, and was thereafter confined to a wheelchair, had to survive for many years while breathing through a ventilator, and said, "Once you choose hope, anything is possible."

CHAPTER THREE

Faith

"Happiness is the meaning and purpose of life, the whole purpose, and end of human existence." - Aristotle

Many prominent philosophers have attempted to address the question, "What causes people to be happy?" World religions, such as Christianity, have attempted to explain how to live a happy, satisfying life by faith, belief in God, reading the Scriptures, adhering to a moral code, and imposing religious dogma.

Buddhism's ideology teaches its adherents how to live a calm and joyful life, which will eventually lead to "salvation." The Dali Lama's best-selling book, The Art of Happiness, discusses how to discover happiness as you go through life. It all starts with a Buddhist conversion.

Positive psychology, which focuses on the science of enjoyment, has emerged as a new topic of research in psychology in recent years. Significant research has been undertaken in this field, and many outstanding books have been created as a result. Martin Seligman, a well-known psychologist, has written two well-known books, "Authentic Happiness" and "Learned Optimism," which show how we might raise our degree of happiness in life.

So, what can we do to make ourselves happy? And how can we make ourselves happy if we are already happy? In this chapter, I'll explain what it means to be happy. I'll also discuss what factors influence our level of happiness. As Seligman advises, I shall also describe three paths to happiness. And I'll outline eight things you may do to boost your happiness in your life.

What exactly is happiness? When you ask different people to define happiness, you will get a variety of answers. Most people have no idea what makes them happy. They are in a condition of automatism, with the automatic pilot turned on. They never consider what makes them happy. They never ponder the meaning and purpose of their lives. They do not enjoy life's pleasures, are not socially linked, and their lives have no profound significance.

Happiness has been characterized as "subjective-well-being" by many positive psychologists. Individuals define happiness as a subjective state. It is a matter of personal preference. It comprises all of the pleasant and good emotions that we experience when we are happy, such as affection, joy, and thankfulness. True happiness, according to many positive psychologists, is more than merely a good emotional state. Subjective well-being has a cognitive or mental component as well. A happy individual is a content with his or her existence. A happy person lives a life that has meaning and purpose. And the contented individual believes that he is living the proper way. This is referred to as "life satisfaction."

So, true happiness is a subjective state in which a person experiences positive emotions such as contentment or thankfulness, as well as a cognitive state in which the person believes he is living a meaningful and purposeful existence.

We are pleased because of various situations and occurrences, such as falling in love, receiving a promotion or raise at work, watching an exciting cricket match, walking on the beach, or winning the lottery.

A person's well-being is influenced in part by their external surroundings. People who work and have some financial goods are happier than destitute people who live under a bridge. People who are healthy are happier than those who are sick with cancer or other ailments. However, a person's well-being is also affected by how he thinks and feels about his living circumstances. Some people, for example, live blissfully in poverty. Some people are happier than healthy persons who are afflicted with terrible illnesses or disorders. Why is this the case? What factors influence our level of happiness? Positive psychologists study what elements contribute to human happiness. The "Happiness Set Point" notion was developed by them. It states that three variables influence a person's happiness: 50% of our happiness is genetically determined; 10% is affected by social factors such as the sensation of being connected to social and economic situations such as making a living, and 40% is determined by how we think and feel about ourselves and our life.

According to theory, we are drawn to a predetermined amount of genetically predetermined bliss. As a result, for various reasons, some people are willing to be happier than others. Perhaps the person was born outgoing or has a more upbeat outlook. Perhaps the individual is gifted with the artistic ability to learn to play the guitar, sing, write, and think creatively.

However, the Happiness Set-Point Theory indicates that when we make the decision to be happy, we can modify our level of happiness, improve it, enhance it, adjust our life to be happier, and take responsibility for raising the degree of happiness. In our daily existence.

Three Approaches to Happiness Martin Seligman, a well-known psychologist, defined three paths to happiness in his book "Authentic Happiness": a joyful life, an engaged life, and meaningful life. He contends that happy people have lives that are full of joy, involvement, and meaning.

There is no doubt that we can find happiness through life's pleasures, such as purchasing a new automobile or a large house, purchasing new clothing or massaging, going to the cottage for summer vacations, or traveling to any far exotic country. A person who lives a pleasurable existence loves sensuous pleasures such as food, sex, rock music, drugs, alcohol, roller coaster rides, and hot baths. Enjoyment as a Path to Happiness is frequently connected with a hedonist, a person who lives by the motto "seeking happiness while avoiding pain." This type of person is preoccupied with enjoying the present moment, often foolishly, while ignoring the long-term ramifications of their activities. This type of individual is frequently caught up in a Hedonic treadmill.

When people seek happiness through rapid gratification and pleasure, they frequently become like rats on a treadmill, always pursuing an exciting relationship, a huge pay at work, flying to an exotic destination, purchasing a big car, or the extreme thrill of their free time. It's similar to smoking marijuana. They are continually developing in terms of novelty and thrill-seeking. For a time, these people are exposed to new content, new activities, or new pleasures as a result of the new person. Happiness, however, is fleeting. This "emotional high" dissipates over time, as does the sense of happiness. So, if you want to be happy through hedonic pleasure, you should seek out and pursue a new type of pleasure on the hedonic treadmill. This type of individual will never be content, joyful, or satisfied.

Hedonic pleasure, according to Seligman, is ephemeral. It will not endure forever. As a result, the individual must find strategies to preserve happiness. Take advantage of the situation. Show off your joy. Remember the occasion. Share your joy with others. Pay attention and hone your comprehension. Make a mental picture of it.

Keep in mind the context of your encounter. Keep your focus on the present moment. Concentrate on the here and now. Meditation can help you become more conscious.

Purge your joys. It counteracts the negative effects of habit on happiness. To put it another way, strive for happiness on a daily basis. Every week, you can discover enjoyable work such as reading a book, walking, or having sex.

Seligman, a psychologist, defined the second level of happiness. He referred to it as "engagement life." When a person takes this path, he or she is said to be tough and involved in many facets of life. The job is understandable. A person, like a close group of friends, has a lot of social support. The individual has a love relationship with the significant other. A spiritual connection exists between a person and a specific faith, religion, belief in God, or supreme force.

The individual is immersed in leisure activities, resulting in a state of flow, a sensation of timelessness in which the person engages in leisure activities, losing all sense of time. Reading, writing, participating in intriguing conversation, shooting photographs, learning to play a musical instrument, or playing in a sport such as tennis or cricket are examples of leisure activities that result in a "flow" experience.

When a person pursues this way to happiness, he or she will be able to transcend himself or herself. The individual has the ability to watch out for themselves while also caring for the well-being of others and the world around them. The individual is empathetic and caring. The individual frequently desires benevolence, or the highest good. Individuals strive to overcome social problems in their society, community, or world. The individual is dedicated to a cause larger than their personal demands and pressures.

How does one find a meaningful life? The person is frequently involved in voluntary work, teaching, and advising. The individual is frequently a volunteer, assisting the less fortunate, those in need of basic food, shelter, and clothing.

According to Seligman, the happiest people are those who have a pleasurable, engaged, and meaningful existence.

Sometimes I have a strong feeling that I am not living in a nihilistic, existential situation, that life has no external significance, happiness, future hope, purpose, or meaning. This deeper meaning became clear to me as I overcome my own personal needs and desires, as well as my own personal concerns about the needs or issues of a stranger, friend, or family member. a member of a community. I've discovered that when I help others, I experience a greater sense of meaning and purpose as if I'm doing something virtuous. When I am empathic and sympathetic to the issues and concerns of others, I feel really joyful and as if I am doing something very valuable and purposeful in my life.

You may be glad for a job, a paycheck, or to be well and disease-free, among other things.

Random acts of kindness, such as laughing at a stranger, leaving the door open, and giving some of your pocket money to a homeless person on the street, should be practiced.

Enjoy life's transient pleasures and delights. In other words, don't waste your life turning on autopilot while traveling down the Highway of Life. Instead of inhaling nice scents, take in the stunning daybreak. Enjoy a passionate kiss, hold hands, and engage in a stimulating conversation with a wonderful friend. Most people live in the present moment. Live in the present moment.

Acquire the ability to forgive people. According to research, it takes more energy to be angry at another person than it does to get rid of our furious thoughts and sentiments. According to studies, when we forgive people, we experience comfort and peace of mind, which leads to contentment.

When we are furious with others, our rage often consumes us. It induces mental anguish. We can't sleep because we're obsessed with vengeance. When we forgive others, we let go of our anger and move on, allowing us to focus our attention and energy on the things in life that bring us joy.

Spend time and attention on friends and family, and maintain good relationships with significant others. According to research, happy people have significant social connections with others. When we have strong, trusted, supporting friendships, when we have close family relationships, when we are close or able to live with a soul mate, and when we have an intimate, warm, good relationship with another person, we are closer to self-actualization.

Take care of both your mind and your body. According to studies, having more energy can make a difference in your life, allowing you to enjoy more activities, such as fitness or sports, or sociability. According to research, when you are active, your self-esteem rises. Regular exercise, according to studies, produces endorphins, a hormone that helps you feel better and boosts the body's relaxation response, making you feel more relaxed. You can take care of your mind and body if you get enough rest and sleep. You can exhibit restraint by not overeating, drinking too much alcohol, or smoking too much marijuana. Every day, you can find some peace and quiet. You can take some time to unwind and rest. You can lift your spirits by reading meaningful poetry, literature, or anything else that interests you. You can meditate to relax your body and mind while also gaining peace and tranquillity.

Create coping techniques for dealing with stress and adversity. You can become a member of a club, an association, or a social support group. You can put money aside for a rainy day. You can prepare for a potential calamity or setback. You can devise a backup strategy. You can find the proper life philosophy for you, such as Buddhism. You can find faith and confidence in God and join the church. You can either learn to employ positive self-talk or learn how to tackle the situation using other coping skills linked with cognitive-behavioral therapy. The ways you employ to deal with stress, difficulty, and issues are limitless. You must track them down.

Gratitude can be expressed in a variety of ways. You can say "thank you" when someone does something nice. Remember a friend's birthday by sending them a card or gift, taking them out for a beer, and wishing them a happy birthday. If you owe someone money, pay it back. If you see anything that makes you happy, cheerful, or grateful, tell the individual why you like it and show your gratitude. If you don't tell someone you love them, they will assume you don't. You don't want to be tormented by the unexpected loss of a loved one, so you don't express your gratitude to them. You must devise strategies for responding. You should also discover ways to convey your appreciation without expecting anything in return.

Happiness is a personal decision that each of us must make for ourselves. Once you've determined to be happy, you must seek out the happiness that is best for you. You must determine what types of people, activities, pleasures, and desires make you happy. Then you must take action to transform your life and welcome joy when it comes knocking.

To be happy, you must cultivate more positive feelings by engaging in activities that promote happiness, joy, thankfulness, intimacy, and so on.

You must make the "correct" decisions in life. You must live the life you desire, which includes choosing a significant work or career, accepting a specific faith and trusting in God, finding someone important to spend your life with, and indulging in leisure activities that both challenge and overwhelm you. ", such as reading a nice book, playing the piano, or painting a landscape.

Whether you enjoy your free time or work your way up the corporate ladder, you must live up to the standards that have been set for you.

A sense of purpose is critical for happiness. Each of us must set our own objectives. A purpose can serve to give your life significance.

According to research, when we grow and develop, we are happier when we learn something new, find satisfaction, extend ourselves, climb the hierarchy of demands in the masses, strive for self-realization, and become the best.

We are happy in order to obtain happiness, not in order to achieve happiness. For example, learning to play the piano is more enjoyable than practicing what you already know. In other words, we discover happiness by immersing ourselves in things, people, and activities that push us, stretch us, require us to spend energy and talent, and mold and reshape us. When we choose happiness, our lives become works of art.

It is the process of working toward a goal, not the goal itself. So, if you're writing a memoir, there's more delight and satisfaction in writing your life story than there is in printing and publishing a book.

You will be happy as a result. You make choices, identify the ones that make you happy, and pursue them every day of your life; you go through the process to completion. Then it doesn't matter since you don't know what happens when you die. But you know you've lived a life worth living, one full of meaning and purpose and joy.

CHAPTER FOUR

How to be resilient?

"When the door to happiness closes, another door opens. But we often stare at a closed-door for a long time and we do not see an open door.

A persistent person can face and overcome problems, failures, misfortunes, sicknesses, tragedies, and the death of a loved one. They can maintain composure when faced with stressful situations and difficulties. A strong man is not a victim. When they are negatively affected, they focus on problem-solving, set goals to overcome the negative, and take action to overcome adversity. They focus on the positive of a sad situation, expecting a better outcome. Resilience is a trait that can be developed with time and effort to learn how to deal with adversity when faced with life and how to move forward and overcome adversity that often causes sadness and anxiety.

Change is part of life. Pain is part of life. The world can be cruel and indifferent. Most people prefer the status quo, but nothing remains the same. There are countless events that cause pain and change.

Death of a loved one, such as a child or spouse. It leads to unemployment, employment, and poverty. Financial problems debt settlement. Diseases and diseases such as cancer. Natural disasters such as earthquakes and tornadoes. An accident that results in injury or worse, disability.

Each of these is an example of a stressful event and negativity. Holmes and Reik developed the scale of life events. The purpose of this scale is to determine the level of stress in an individual's life and to indicate the effect of stress on the individual's physical and mental health. Death, divorce, injury, illness, and job loss are just some of life's stressors. When a person experiences and copes with one or more of these life problems at any given time, they are at risk of becoming mentally or physically ill.

Resilient people are optimistic about the future even under adverse circumstances and can take steps to overcome and overcome these stressful life events.

Who are the stable people? People react differently when tragedy or misfortune hits their faces. Some are depressed and unable to bear it. They are addicted to drugs, alcohol, anger, anxiety, depression, and slow recovery from misfortune. Others will grow and cope with the occasion, deal with setbacks and move on with their lives. These kinds of people know that challenges, setbacks, obstacles, dangers, even tragedy are qualities of the human condition. They recognize that pain and sorrow are part of life. They have the property of elasticity.

The Express looks optimistic about the future. An optimist believes that the future is bright and those good things will happen, that he will overcome ups and downs, obstacles and adversity, and work hard to achieve his goals and dreams. Optimists are not blind to ignore the negative. Optimism means focusing on the positive side of a curious event or situation while recognizing the negative side. Optimism is finding the best way out of a bad situation. Hope arises when a person thinks with optimism.

They have strong social support networks such as friends, family, and soulmates. In difficult times, a persistent person seeks help and advice from a trusted person.

They have solid critical thinking abilities. Tough individuals find ways to tackle their concerns.

They have self-appreciation inspiration. Durable individuals have an uplifting perspective towards themselves. They for the most part feel certain, which adds to their feeling of control. They accept that their activities will decidedly influence the result of a terrible circumstance.

Set and attempt to accomplish the objective. At the point when difficulty comes out of the blue, versatile people foster an activity plan that has a bunch of objectives to address a mishap or setback.

They gain from difficulty. The hopeful person gains from difficulty and utilizations this information to manage future mishaps, difficulties, and setbacks.

CHAPTER FIVE

Overcoming fatigue

"Aren't life multiple times more limited than we get exhausted of ourselves?" - Frederick Nietzsche

What is fatigue? An inclination can regularly be capable when we sit idle or lose interest in the individual, circumstance, place, movement. Our psyche begins to meander, perhaps fantasizing. We can't center. Then, at that point, we understand that we have lost interest - that we can't concentrate. We frequently need to escape from weariness yet can't. Feeling nauseated, overlooking our environmental factors, we normally yawn.

Weariness is a typical indication of the human condition. Over the long haul, we regularly get exhausted with our accomplices, exhausted with our work, exhausted with the schedules of our lives. Assuming we feel anything, it turns out to be more normal, so we adorn our homes, purchase new vehicles, and travel to extraordinary objections. Youngsters lose interest in school and look for interruptions. Ladies who telecommute are exhausted with housework, preparing similar suppers, looking for food, and needing to set off for college or work. Travelers regularly get exhausted from dealing with a similar street and afterward stall out in rush hour gridlock, so they call their mates or pay attention to book recordings or recreation music. Customers hang tight in line to pay for their food and get exhausted and restless or discombobulated. Notwithstanding TV, motion pictures, computer games, and cell phones, fatigue is an omnipresent element of current life.

Plenty of profound masterminds and imaginative scholars have expounded on the real factors of weariness. Creator Margaret George gives a fascinating portrayal: "Weariness is a horrendously useless condition, and the medication that can tackle it - that is, movement - looks sickening. Arrow-based weaponry? It is freezing and, additionally, requires re-covering the garments; The rodents were at the grass. Music? Is nauseating to hear; To create this, a ton is burdened. Etc. Of all the anguish, weariness is at last heartless. Eventually, it transforms you into an extraordinary man who sits idle - a relative of lethargy and a sibling of distress. "

Improvement of free air like white dividers and no workmanship office. Rehashing an errand, maybe chipping away at a mechanical production system. Carefulness, in which an individual needs to center, for instance, sitting in chapel and paying attention to a message.

Impassive fatigue. It is unwinding, fun, passionate in light of a circumstance where you want to do anything. For instance, after numerous days at work, you return home, relax in a sluggish kid's seat, turn on the TV, and dream about watching a sitcom apathetically.

Adjusting weariness. You are in a circumstance where you would rather not be. Perhaps you need to get away and contemplate every one of the elective exercises you experience.

Looking for weariness. You are anxious, need interruptions, or need to change your current circumstance. Perhaps you feel dull and trapped in work and fantasy about tracking down something else and better. Possibly your relationship has lost its enthusiasm and presently you need a new thing and unique.

Response weariness. You are caught and discouraged - and incapable to get away from the circumstance. For instance, youngsters in state-funded schools regularly experience this sort of fatigue. Rather than having a great time on the swings or slides, they ought to pay attention to the educator who gives directions on the spelling.

Indifference and boredom. You feel relaxed, withdrawn, and indifferent to the world around you. Maybe you just read the morning newspaper, drink coffee, and sit on the terrace engaged in your daily routine, and the news feels just as boring. This event seems to have been experienced before.

What happens if you get bored? Much: Our minds get faster and our times get slower. As our heart rate increases, the body releases the stress hormone cortisol into the bloodstream. Boredom can be relaxing, but otherwise, it can be stressful, especially if a person experiences it too much.

And boredom leads to actions that destroy our health, security, success, and happiness. Most people eat when they are bored, which leads to obesity. Some people get into the habit of avoiding boredom by using too many illegal drugs and drinking too much alcohol. Endless boredom can make you tired, indifferent, and frustrated. At school, children are taught to be calm and compassionate. Some children find it boring, unfocused, and difficult to study.

Some people have to work boringly, which reduces their motivation and leads to poor performance and absenteeism. For those who are bored, life often feels meaningless and purposeless, which can lead to anxiety, depression, and substance and alcohol abuse. Many bored people engage in dangerous behaviors such as B. Unprotected sex, non-marriage sex, sex with prostitutes, sex with multiple partners. Participants in unprotected sex can get sexually transmitted diseases such as HIV. Researchers have discovered that the boredom of teenagers can lead to destruction, riots, and hooligans. Those looking for thrills who are tired of their daily lives take high-risk actions such as skydiving from planes, driving at high speeds, and climbing steep rocky mountains. Many thrill-seekers have died because of their misfortunes.

Remedies for boredom are often a personal choice. We choose a boring life by being indifferent to our circumstances. Or we do not know how to escape boredom and do not try to learn. At other times, we can not get out of the situation of boredom, so we get stuck in boredom. Many people use their smartphones when they are bored. This is a short-term fix and is not always an option, especially if you cannot use your digital gadget in a particular location. How can we keep our lives interesting?

When you imagine a boring situation, plan to divert your attention. For example, solve a crossword puzzle in a clinic or a sudoku puzzle in a newspaper. When you know you have to wait, bring a good book or newspaper and read while waiting.

Learn a new skill. Do you have any dreams? Desires? Desires? Bring anything fascinating and fun, whether it's piano, creative writing, digital photography, or ballroom dancing. Talk to others. Have fun, spend time with friends who like to do new things, are fascinating, and see life as an adventure.

Make fitness a part of your daily life. Join the fitness program you enjoy. Some people like to train alone. Yoga, weight training, walking, jogging, and swimming are some of the activities you can do yourself. Others enjoy being with others and joining groups. Activities that you can do with others, such as squash, tennis, hockey, baseball, bowling, and more.

Please suit your taste. What are you enjoying? Do you have a dream? Take steps to make it come true. Suppose you dream of becoming a published author. You can start writing in a journal. After that, I took some creative writing classes. Then read poetry, fiction, and creative nonfiction.

Change your environment. For example, if you are bored in your office, find a new job. If you are bored with your courses at university, enroll in others. If your house is dull and dull, add another color to it and hang a painting or photograph.

Break the routines of your daily life. In other words, do something new. Make new friends, pursue new ways of working, eat at new restaurants, watch new movies, watch new shows on TV.

Be creative. Everyone is somehow creative, but many say, "I'm not creative." This negative thinking prevents us from taking steps to lead a creative life. You can overcome this creative block by engaging in creative activities. You can visit art galleries, watch rock concerts, and buy movie tickets. Anyone skilled in the art can start sketching, drawing, painting, engraving, and photography. If you don't know how to enroll in some art classes or read books and magazines to learn.

Find the answer to your curiosity. The desire to know more about everything. There are many ways to get the answer. Reading about topics is a good way to learn. The other is immersing yourself in new experiences, such as moving to a new city where you can learn about culture, cooking, art, and people. Searching for your answer on the internet is another. Enrolling in a course aimed at becoming a subject expert is a common way to satisfy your hungry curiosity. American writer and poet Dorothy Parker once said, "The cure for boredom is curiosity. You can't heal your curiosity."

Note. Use your senses to find out what's happening at the moment. What do you see? I want to hear? felt? smell? taste? Create a mental note. Write the details in a notebook or journal. Take some pictures with your smartphone. When careful, focus your attention on the creative aspects of line, shape, form, texture, earth color. Most public spaces and people can become interesting by observing the details. The artist, Andy Warhol, once said, "Usually the little things that bother you should not let you suddenly be thrilled."

Learn to meditate. Once you've learned, make meditation a way to deal with boring experiences. Let's say you find yourself in an inevitable and boring place. Perhaps you're stuck in the dentist's waiting room and you're starting to get bored. Close your eyes, meditate and focus on your breathing. It clears and calms your mind and helps you develop inner peace. Participate in the

streaming experience. Flow is a state of mind, a positive emotion that contributes to personal well-being. The experience sets the mood and rewards you for wanting to do it again, as you become absorbed in the experience and lose all traces of time. Mihari Six Gent Positive psychologists like Mihari call this the psychology of the right experience. You have to concentrate. You also need to participate in a rewarding and achievable experience that has goals. The experience is also internally rewarding. Immerse yourself in yourself while experiencing a timeless experience. You get feedback from experience and you have control. The flow is usually for activities that you really enjoy, immerse, be happy, lose confidence, enrich, reward, etc., such as writing, painting, running, dancing, etc. It is related.

Annoying Libra is always rational, emotionally vulnerable, very passionate, and maybe a little too strong. Boredom is an unwanted state of mind that we often escape from. If you are bored, change the aspects of your life that make you bored. You can always divert your attention from boredom. Arthur Schopenhauer once said, "Pain and boredom are two enemies of human well-being." By eliminating or reducing the amount of time you get bored, you increase your well-being, life satisfaction, and happiness.

CHAPTER SIX

Finding the Flow of Life

"Happiness is something that each person must individually prepare, nurture and protect."

Wealth, power, gender, and material comfort guarantee happiness and happiness. Not. Many who have the pitfalls of this success are still living a quiet, desperate, empty life, often a fluid experience is not part of their life. What is a flow?

According to Mihari, a professor of psychology and psychiatrist, the flow is the right experience or "complete involvement with life." It's not a goal, but it's a tool people use to immerse themselves in an activity, event, or experience. "At that time, it hit us. The experience is goal-oriented, internally rich, rewarding, and fun. Writing, making art, dancing, playing musical instruments, participating in tennis and chess games. Various activities such as doing create a flow

You can find a flowing experience and use it to transform a purposeless, meaningless, or boring existence into a life of joy, desire, inspiration. A life that enhances your sense of happiness and happiness to change rations and excitement.

There are countless streaming experiences that can enhance your well-being. Feel the flow. When engaging in life experiences that require the use of one or more senses, such as B. Hearing, you can enjoy paying attention to beautiful music.

The flow of socialization. Spend valuable time with others such as B. Interesting conversations with friends, family, and important people.

The river of mankind. Overcome your "self" and help those in need. Both Gandhi and Mother Teresa focused on living a compassionate life and relieving the suffering of others. The flow of the body. Use your body for physical activities such as yoga, running, cycling, dancing, swimming, and sex. Workflow. Using your mind in challenging, internally rewarding work.

Resting flow. Participate in leisure activities that make you think and concentrate, such as hanging on the wall of an art gallery, admiring the wonder of one`s painting. Watching TV is not a streaming experience.

The flow of the spirit. Achieve goals with your mind-read, write, play chess, solve crossword puzzles, sudoku, and other puzzles. What are the obstacles to experiencing the

flow? there are many:

boring. The mediocrity of everyday, repetitive and meaningless experiences can distract you and prevent you from experiencing the flow.

stress. Fear, worry, and anxiety can distract you and deplete the mental energy needed to experience the flow. Alienation, Feeling socially isolated and separated from the hustle and bustle of society can hinder the flow.

Distraction. Noise multitasks, anxiety, responsibilities, etc., destroy the flow. Lack of motivation. Feeling lethargic prevents you from taking steps to experience the flow. Misfortune, sorrow, loss. Each of these drains energy from the mind and body, making it harder to experience the flow.

Daily necessities — lack of food, housing, and clothing. Before you can experience the flow, you need to have a basic standard of living and not have the basic necessities of life. Otherwise, instead of needing flows, focus on meeting those needs.

Attention Deficit Disorders or addictions cause a loss of concentration and you will not be able to experience the flow and its benefits. Each of these distracts, prevents concentration, and fully concentrates on the immediate experience, leading to a perfect experience.

Some people are able to overcome setbacks or challenges, learn from them and turn them into flowing experiences. For example, in coping with stress, people use their psychological resources, social support, and various coping strategies such as problem-solving, goal setting, and stress management.

How can you add flow to your life? Follow your happiness or embrace your desires. Set and work to achieve meaningful goals. Talk to funny, talkative, humorous, and sociable people. Get the art. You can visit the art gallery, learn to play musical instruments and take pictures. Learn new skills. Most people take courses such as creative writing, hands-on learning such as cooking, and learning a new language. Make learning a lifelong pursuit. Add fitness activities that create flow into your life like running, yoga, dancing.

Finding your life goal and taking action to achieve it is crucial. It gives you meaning.

CHAPTER SEVEN

Happiness

"The characterizing normal for doubters is that they accept that awful occasions will proceed for quite a while, that each move they make will be their own issue. It is accepted that the causes are restricted to this one case. "- Positive Analyst

The longing to be content, the craving to purchase a BMW auto, the glow and rest in the poolside in the daylight, the lottery ticket, or the acquisition of another pair of planner Levis generally trigger human exercises. Energetic kiss. Pascal said, "Joy is the longing of each person for each activity, and surprisingly the individuals who are hanged." In his success The Craft of Joy, the Dalai Lama expressed: "I accept that the reason for life is to look for joy. That is clear. Whether or not somebody has confidence in religion ... we as a whole need something great throughout everyday life. Thus, I think our lives are moving towards satisfaction as it were. "

Bliss is the sensation of happiness or fulfillment. I'm not alluding to temporary pleasurable minutes or little encounters of delight, yet an enduring feeling of fulfillment and fulfillment in one's life. This longing to be content inspires quite a large number. Being cheerful is the importance and reason for human life. The vast majority don't share with themselves, "I will do either or something so I can be blissful." All things being equal, the quest for satisfaction by implication happens as one continued looking for joy or fulfilling encounters.

As per research in certain brain science, we have command over the vast majority of our joy. To do as such, we should find ways to build our fulfillment and satisfaction. It says that just 10% of our still up in the air by the gig we appreciate, the affection for a perfect partner, having a lot of cash in a financial balance, and actual delights like a games vehicle. Another half not set in stone acquired and outside our ability to control. For instance, an individual with inherited DNA for schizophrenia, bipolar confusion, uneasiness, or wretchedness might find it harder to encounter fulfillment and satisfaction in life than somebody brought into the world with a hopeful character. Positive therapists allude to this hereditarily foreordained degree of joy as the "set point" of our satisfaction. The excess 40% of joy is influenced quite a bit by. We can decide to not accomplish anything or work to build our feeling of joy.

There are numerous ways we can decide to be content. The main choice should be to change our disposition and work on raising our degree of joy - our degree of bliss and fulfillment. It should be a cognizant decision rather than a thoughtless walk around life asking why we are distraught.

Perhaps the most straightforward advance you can take to change your disposition is to zero in on being happy with what you have. At the end of the day, be grateful for the gifts you as of now have, like great wellbeing, a task that covers your bills, and somebody who loves you. Zeroing in on what you as of now have consistently diminishes the craving for a novel, new thing, unique, and more pleasant, which frequently prompts disappointment. Positive therapists recommend that you set up a Thanksgiving magazine. A few times each week, you record what you are appreciative of having. Consistently, I'm helped to remember that it is so gainful to be healthy.

Another progression you can take (a Buddhist practice) is to live astutely. Rather than zeroing in your psyche on the obscure future, maybe stressing or expecting catastrophe or zeroing in on the dismal memory from before, you will concentrate at this very moment. "The genuine bliss is in partaking in the present," said scholar Seneca.

Living astutely is difficult. You need to prepare your brain. The most effective way to prepare your psyche is to rehearse care contemplation. You can likewise tune your faculties - sight, smell, taste, contact, hearing, and feeling. For instance, assuming that you plunk down and turn on the sound system and pay attention to helpful music, you are living keenly. Be that as it may, assuming you plunk down, turn on the sound system and begin perusing the paper, you are not. In this way, another way you can become more intelligent is to do each undertaking in turn. Assuming that you accomplish more than a certain something, you are diverting yourself. This isn't caring. To be cautious, you want to concentrate on what's going on at this very moment.

For some, the longing to be content by encountering joy and satisfaction is the significance and motivation behind life. The longing to feel delight and fulfillment likewise persuades numerous to make a move. Sigmund Freud, a main figure in brain science, contended that we want to encounter joy, which thusly inspires us.

The issue with needing a libertine life loaded up with simple pleasurable pursuits is that satisfaction is passing.

We experience satisfaction for some time and it vanishes, so we should continually look for new encounters that fill our lives with delight. Generally wonderful encounters have the advantage of lessening - the more charming experience we have, the more straightforward it is to get exhausted, the less we want. Bliss is likewise vaporous - it vanishes. Thus, we are continually keeping watch for new fun encounters.

The other possible issue with joy is that it can set off glut rather than control. For instance, following a long, distressing day at work, an individual might skirt six or seven containers of lager and begin getting a charge out of a couple of jugs of blend. In the wake of encountering the joys of sex and sexual peak, a man needs to encounter sexual joy from however many delightful ladies as would be prudent rather than sharing his craving for sexual joy and fulfillment with a perfect partner, maybe with his better half. An individual might need the flavor of the food and the solace it offers. Rather than eating with some restraint, the individual eats himself into corpulence and afterward experiences a coronary failure, which makes him carry on with an existence of incapacity. Along these lines, needing just lovely encounters will neglect to give a long period of joy.

We can have a commitment life by partaking in exercises or encounters that make a perspective called "stream". We are at this point not unsure, zeroed in within, agonizing over the future or being annoyed by the past. We know how we are treating the present. Time stops when we are in inflow. We experience this perspective through compensating work/vocation and sporting exercises, maybe playing exploratory writing or playing an instrument or taking road photos.

Rather than living alone, we look for the existence of commitment by developing companionship. We do this for an assortment of reasons, maybe somebody to partake in the delights of life, somebody to help socially, somebody to appreciate the great discussion, to share a few chuckles ....

We likewise need love. Love is a fundamental human need, for example, food-safe house and security. The greater part of mankind needs to be adored and treasured. To encounter the advantages of affection, an individual should be occupied with life, not living alone. Besides, love seldom prospers and suffers in the event that we don't develop our object of affection. To be cherished by someone else, we should give within recent memory, exertion, and consideration. We want to rehearse the language of adoration, invest quality energy, impart expressions of fondness, and give actual touch. Should be self and providing for one another. Without one another adoration evaporates and kicks the bucket. To that end, most relationships bomb everyday hardship.

As indicated by research in sure brain science, we can work on our degree of bliss by making an existence with importance and reason. Significance is frequently pursued by taking on a specific conviction. An individual understands sacred text, goes to higher powers, acknowledges a gathering of strict convictions, takes the visually impaired animosity of the confidence since it expands their profound appetite, decreases the feeling of dread toward death, and answers inquiries concerning the incredible secrets of life. Is there a Divine being? For sure occurs after I kick the bucket?

We additionally make importance and reason by defining objectives and chipping away at accomplishing them, maybe getting a college degree, composing a novel, running a long-distance race, making professional progress. Michel de Montaigne, "The best and most grand show-stopper of man is to live with reason."

Along these lines, by adjusting our point of view and choosing to be happy with what we as of now have, we can expand our feeling of fulfillment towards life, which upgrades our feeling of bliss. Consequently, we should remember our good fortune. Additionally, one should figure out how to zero in the psyche on living shrewdly right now. We can work on our degree of daily routine fulfillment by filling our experiences with happiness, stream, love, companionship, significance and reason.

CHAPTER EIGHT

Despondency

The misfortune incites despondency. Furthermore, sadness appears as mental torment and enduring, pain, despondency, mental torment. The most remarkable type of misfortune is the passing of a friend or family member. A portion of different kinds of anguish that can cause melancholy is separate, employment cutback, the demise of a pet, the finish of companionship, or loss of monetary security.

Misfortune frequently transforms one's self-appreciation and lifestyle. For instance, when an individual is terminated, the person in question loses their personality (assuming the character is connected to work), status, relational connections, and schedule. Anguish is general - everybody encounters at least one episode of sadness in the course of their life. So, anguish is a manifestation of the human condition.

Misery is additionally private. Individuals respond distinctively to losing. Certain individuals are furious, express their annoyance nonsensically, and most likely shout at their life partner. Certain individuals abstain from torment and enduring by consuming an excessive amount of alcohol or unlawful medications. Others devote their lives to hecticness. Rather than investing in some opportunity to lament, the individual devotes themselves to the work. Anyway, others are occupied with enchanted reasoning, which is a type of unreasonable thinking where an individual accepts that something has occurred for some off-base explanation.

Itinerant species. The individual communicates numerous feelings like resentment, dismissal, disarray. The individual's sorrow isn't settled and the individual neglects to see what it means for their life.

Memorialist. The dispossessed individual centers their time and energy on safeguarding the memory of the expired, for example, making workmanship for her feelings, making a landmark, composing a sonnet, and composing verses for pretty much nothing.

Normalizer. The lamenting individual tries to supplant what the person in question has lost by zeroing in on keeping up with or fortifying social binds with family, companions, significant other, or local area.

Dissident. The lamenting individual tracks down importance from the misfortune by utilizing their insight to help other people, for example, chipping in or tracking down another business way in helping other people.

Searcher. The lamenting individual looks outside to comprehend his misfortune. The individual frequently encounters existential tension. To respond to their inquiries, the individual goes to confidence, reasoning, and otherworldliness.

Misery has no period to leave one's life. Certain individuals lament for a couple of days or weeks; Others experience misfortune for a long time. For some, sorrow vanishes like a mist in the daylight. Each individual experiencing pain should see as their specific manner back out of the chasm. The lamenting individual goes to companions for basic encouragement. They share their sorrow with a confided companion who offers solace and consolation. Others are leaned towards confidence. The lamenting individual responds to their inquiries regarding the misfortune, tracks down the comfort, and figures out how to acknowledge the misfortune by perusing the sacred writings, conversing with the cleric, and petitioning God.

Pain has no period to leave one's life. Certain individuals lament for a couple of days or weeks; Others experience misfortune for a long time. For some, sadness vanishes like a haze in the daylight. Each experiencing melancholy should see as their specific manner back from the pit. The lamenting individual goes to companions for everyday encouragement. They share their pain with a confided companion who offers solace and consolation. Others are leaned towards confidence. The lamenting individual responds to their inquiries regarding the misfortune, tracks down the comfort, and figures out how to acknowledge the misfortune by perusing the sacred texts, conversing with the minister, and imploring God.

Craftsmanship has additionally turned into a famous technique for managing distress. Many individuals resort to the workmanship as a type of treatment. Psychological well-being experts additionally use craftsmanship treatment as a treatment to battle and recuperate from misery. There is an assortment of workmanship treatments, for example, making a misery cover with mud; Drawing or portraying your feelings, considerations, recollections, encounters of melancholy; Or making a scrapbook of the memory of the perished; Gathering pictures and making a photograph collection.

Others put their pen to paper and record their contemplations, sentiments, encounters, and lost recollections in the Diary of Distress. Composing can be pretty much as invigorating as sympathizing with your aggravation with an advisor.

Certain individuals take part in an exhausting activities like running cycling or swimming. Actual exercise can lessen pressure and assist with disposing of sensations of outrage. Many hug yoga and contemplation. These otherworldly practices clear the psyche from quietness and stress.

The vast majority will more often than not work and spotlight on it without permitting themselves to endure misfortune. This most frequently applies to a not individual have an obsessive worker, the balance between fun and serious activities.

For others, sadness can cause them to feel discouraged. To escape the pit of trouble, these individuals need antidepressants and/or talk treatment.

Melancholy is important for the human condition. We can never escape from misery. Misery is concealed in the shadows of our valuable lives, standing by to assault us when we wouldn't dare hope anymore. Regardless of the amount we set ourselves up for misfortune, we can't completely shield ourselves from the blows of sadness or defeated distress without allowing ourselves to recuperate from the aggravation and experiencing brought about by critical misfortune.

CHAPTER NINE

Straightforward

I accept many individuals accept that a typical individual is immaculate, not deranged or actually incapacitated. I accept it is normal for some individuals to embrace a "human condition" like love, regard, and opportunity for family and the local area. They additionally desire to make progress, harmony, satisfaction, and bliss, - - and to be liberated from agony and languishing. Whenever asked what is normal, the vast majority offer a response that upholds business, as usual, customary insight, and crowd mindset.

A culture that figures out what makes an individual's life typical and remarkable. Sociologists allude to this as "social relativity". This is valid and "typical or alluring" alludes to the way of life wherein an individual lives. Assessment and hypothesis that an individual's qualities, mentalities, convictions, conduct, design, objectives, dreams, and so forth ought to be perceived by others as far as the way of life wherein that individual lives. Culture changes an individual socially to embrace laid out qualities, convictions, accepted practices, laws, and requests. Moreover, good and bad, moral or shameless, attractive or unwanted reasoning is connected with culture. For instance, in most Islamic nations, ladies are relied upon to cover their appearances and bodies with a cloak. Not wearing a veil is wrongdoing and rude. Notwithstanding, in Western majority rules systems, ladies who wear the "veil" are frequently viewed as mistreated, compliant, in reverse, and boorish.

There are numerous associations that assist with characterizing shared traits like family, school, religion, police and the overall set of laws, broad communications. In a family, kids gain from their folks what is correct and what's going on, ordinary or unwanted. In an ordinary family, when a youngster accomplishes something wrong, the person in question will be rebuffed. The educational system mingles the understudy to take on explicit qualities, information and conduct. Assuming that an understudy beats one more kid on school premises, the person will frequently be condemned or rebuffed by the head. Assuming an understudy utilizes words that are rude, like saying "fuck off" to the educator, the individual in question is typically rebuffed with suspension. Different understudies see the hardest understudy "in an unexpected way" than the group. All religions show their herd moral code, and that implies you should not kill, submit infidelity, falsehood, or take. The police power authorizes the rule of law. Assuming an individual disregards the law, the person will be accused of a criminal offense. On the off chance that the wrongdoing is significant, maybe assuming the blamed loots the save money with a handgun, the individual will be locked in the slammer until a preliminary can occur. The courts will decide if they are "correct" and "wrong," "ordinary" or "exceptional," and convict the culprits of the offense.

I recommend we as a whole have a clouded side or shade. Along these lines, not a solitary one of us are "ordinary". Put somebody at serious risk - and their horrendous apprehensions or undesirable motivations will come out. For instance, standard men perpetrate monstrosities in the midst of contention. Some would contend that this is the "ordinariness of wickedness" we as a whole have. We might be associated to submit abhorrent demonstrations, as well as to be not interested in it. Our adapted mentalities shape our great and terrible convictions as well as our activities. We are associated through broad communications to "disdain the adversary". Simply partake in the fight. In any case, murder is legitimized all the time.

Thinking back ever, I recollect what the Americans did with the A-bomb on Hiroshima. Over the long haul, I accept this act is one of the most ruthless demonstrations of current man. Likewise, read the set of experiences books in Western nations and you read the "legitimization" for killing blameless individuals. Disregarding the desire to rebuff and tracking down one more method for giving up persuasively is an uncommon demonstration. The public authority and the broad communications look to make steadfast positive energy at any expense. Disdain towards the foe turns into the "new standard." Yet has it at any point been effective? Not a chance. For that reason, the nuclear bomb was never dropped from WWII. Men should fall back on exceptional arrangements and conduct to track down tranquil arrangements.

I accept we as a whole have a public character and a private character. We show public character on the "public life stage", in the workplace, at family social affairs, in the chapel, driving a vehicle, etc. Our public character by and large takes on "the state of affairs", the accepted practices, the laws of society. Our own character is presented to individuals we trust, like companions, family, and sweethearts. It is our "clouded side" or "shadow", some bothersome character characteristic that is uncovered during troublesome, struggle, stress, or difficulty, for instance, when an individual loses his employment and ends up being furious or begins drinking intensely. The issue to be addressed.

CHAPTER TEN

Concern of existentialism

Existentialism is a philosophy concerned with discovering the meaning and purpose of life and self through free will, choice and personal responsibility. We have the freedom to choose, yet the values and morals imposed by society cause conflict in the mind. So, we are not free like a commotion flying in the sky.

Existence precedes essence. In other words, each person determines his or her own values about work, leisure, sex, love, family, faith, spirituality, abortion, capital punishment, euthanasia, and so on, and each person defines his or her own morality, what is right or wrong, what is moral or Immoral, what is good and bad behavior. It was not provided as a gift from God.

Each individual is socialized to adopt a specific definition of morality by family, by religion, by mass media, by law and order. Each person decides for himself what to accept or ignore. When a person is born, he or she has no self, identity, values. They are obtained by living in society.

When we die, our bodies decompose and turn to dust in the air. Does the soul live forever? Does the sense of "self" live on? Or, are we born again? Or, existence, emptiness

— no memory, consciousness, feeling, sight, smell, taste, touch, hearing? Is it null only?

Life is intertwined with fleeting moments of joy. Life means pleasure, sex, booze, drugs, vulgarity. Life is a flow. Life is success and achievement. Life is full of setbacks and obstacles. Life is a struggle. Life is short. If there is nothing after that, is the struggle to conform and achieve it worth it?

CHAPTER ELEVEN

What is that?

We frequently squander a great deal of energy attempting to control our own lives and others. We stress over the obscure future. We attempt to make requests in our own lives and we need others to act as we anticipate. The truth of the matter is that the surprising generally occurs throughout everyday life. The truth of life is that every one of us has the opportunity to settle on our own choices and to go about as we wish. A great many people generally attempt to do how they need - except if they treat, discipline or dread an accidental result.

CHAPTER TWELVE

Living in harmony

Numerous unforeseen occasions and individual encounters undermine our inward feeling of harmony. For instance, the abrupt passing of a friend or family member, unforeseen employment misfortune, stressing over monetary weight, contending with a mate, being truly sick, driving like a lunatic, the essence of an odder who permits you to open the entryway - these occasions can change a quiet brain into a quiet, quiet lake, resembles the ocean. Whenever we are disturbed, our perspective is quiet, and instead of quiet are nervous, dread, outrage, and even displeasure.

The improvement of internal harmony comes from the inside - the perspective of inward harmony - peacefulness and balance and restriction. Every one of us should settle on a choice to live in harmony and afterward center around creating and keeping a quiet perspective.

There are dependably dangers to world harmony and security or worldwide clash. At any crossroads in world history, for some, the proceeding with the danger of common conflict, highway fighting, denials of basic liberties, decimation, dictator states threatening their own residents, atomic conflict and the annihilation of mankind, and as of late, the fanaticism of the individuals who embrace a vote based system, the market economy, opportunity, and equity Turned into the adversary. These dangers and clashes make outrage, disdain, doubt, uneasiness, and dread with the psyche of mankind. These dangers and clashes can likewise prompt generalizations, bias, and prejudice.

There are many advantages to living in harmony. The following are three: First, harmony is an activity we use to foster our otherworldly nature. Second, a quiet life further develops our life fulfillment, bliss, and prosperity. Third, supporting worldwide causes and pioneers advancing harmony instead of fighting will keep the world from falling into a condition of atomic obliteration.

To live in harmony every one of us should develop a serene mental state, not reprisal, and embrace world harmony, not war. "Tit for tat makes the entire world visually impaired," Gandhi once said.

CHAPTER THIRTEEN

Humor

Humor is anything that evokes a smile, fun or laughter. We find humor everywhere. Fat man and slender woman walking with arms outstretched. Someone is having dinner like a pig at the crib. Shapeless people are watching you engage in sex on porn. Someone in a comedy club is listening to an obscene joke. Laughing at our stupidity. Humor is everywhere.

Humor is the best medicine and the easiest way to enjoy life. It is one of the simplest pleasures of life. It is also a desired personality trait. Most people will tell you that they like people who are funny and do not always take life seriously. Not everyone has humor though. Most people do not know life or how to laugh at themselves.

What makes us laugh? It depends. Humor is subjective. In other words, what makes a person laugh is based on personal taste, which is influenced by morality, norms, values, culture, education, religion, and so on. I thought it was funny, you might not. And why did you find it ridiculous, I may not be.

I don't even care about shock humor. You can experience it in "comedy clubs". It is a type of humor that uses taboo sketches about stand-up comic pornography, "gross-out" jokes, x-rated anecdotes, and what many consider to be the limit. For many years, Dad was a stand-up comic in our family.

Even black comedy is not limited to me. The forbidden things of religion and death and the things that many people see as serious things like politicians are bound to make you laugh. Other popular themes are sex, illness, depression, sexual dysfunction, war, addiction, disease.

There are many benefits of humor. Laughter improves your health. It lowers blood pressure, boosts the immune system, reduces pain and suffering, relaxes us, and reduces stress that can lead to mental and physical illness. Humor is often the best medicine. Learning to laugh again for those suffering from depression is the antidote to afternoon ghosts.

Stress kills — so developing and maintaining humor can help you deal with and adapt to life's adversities such as illness, unemployment, disaster and death. Bill Cosby said, "Through humor, you can soften some of life's worst blows. And once you have a laugh, no matter how painful your condition is, you can survive it.

Humor makes us playful and makes life enjoyable. It helps us to be more abrupt, to let go of our defenses, to let go of our obstacles, to become our true person. Humor is an element of happiness. Laughter releases endorphins that make us feel good. It's like a drug that brings us to life.

Humor in the workplace boosts the morale of colleagues and improves the productivity of work. Humor can reduce conflict in a relationship, forming bonds even in difficult, unbearable times if not for humor. Humor can foster friendship, allowing strangers to find a common emotional connection and bond from humor.

Humor makes us see our own flaws or stupidity. It motivates us to change our perspective and see things from a different, funny perspective.

Humor is an attractive personality trait. Check out the profile on the social networking website Like Plenty Fish and you will find that most men and women are looking for someone with a sense of humor. It can not only disarm the person who cares about you, but also communicate amicably, reducing stressful situations, making people feel that you are "easy".

Each of us has the ability to make jokes. Yet many people have given up their humor, perhaps in old age, illness, fatal illness. There is nothing worse than a person who does not have humor, or who does not laugh. Life can be so intense without having to deal with people who don't like or don't like to laugh.

CHAPTER FOURTEEN

Partition from pessimism

Consistently in our lives, we are overpowered with misfortune. Perusing the paper, we find out with regards to the new death, the conflict in the Center East, and insignificant demonstrations of psychological oppression. While heading to work, we see a man on the uncontrollable anger or a Dismissive driver hurrying into our path without a sign.

We hear the killing of the hosts on live radio. We hear the news for the discouraging hour on the radio - the financial exchange crash, another voracious corporate world class middle class criminal or somebody acting like a government official.

At work, we frequently need to manage the consistent grumblings of disappointed collaborators, like low wages, high responsibility, domineering manager, and helpless mentalities. Loved ones feel overpowered by the pressure of their lives - covering bills, bringing up youngsters, and really focusing on older guardians.

This cynicism isn't really great for our emotional wellness. It is an assault on our inner serenity. It defiles the psyche with pictures and musings of despondency. It makes pressure and debilitates our prosperity. More terrible, antagonism makes tension and despondency.

Separating from pessimistic individuals. Certain individuals continually whine about everything or continually scrutinize others. This cynicism obliterates our inspirational perspective on life and harms our confidence. To battle them, we can invest less energy with them or cut them out. I center around associating with positive individuals and individuals with an awareness of what's actually funny and plan ahead with idealism.

Infusing quiet into life. The prevailing message of the media is negative. It investigates war, demise, misfortune, wrongdoing, natural issues - all parts of mankind and the world. Many accept that the Worldwide Town is an unfriendly and impassive spot and the media has mingled us to embrace this view. At the point when the news is discouraging, I transform the channel into a sitcom, transform the radio broadcast into music, watch articles about murder, war and illegal intimidation before or read significant and positive ones.

Leaving it and continuing on. The Beatles sang "Let It Be," yet Buddhists train us to surrender it. Permitting implies permitting the game to play without impeding an unfavorable occasion. Now and again we can bring extra mischief by interceding or exacerbate things. Relinquishing it implies losing our annoyance or disdain. Before, when individuals grumbled, scrutinized or irritated me, I would frequently feel furious or angry and hold my antagonism towards them. Buddhist insight trained me to leave. It will require some investment, however it very well may be accomplished. Reflection is an extraordinary method for disposing of pessimism in the brain. Zeroing in on the current second is another. We can't change the past however we can gain from it. Moreover, on the off chance that we don't relinquish the past, it regularly makes us miserable.

Declining to react to difficulty. Famous subjects of discussion like religion, sex and legislative issues. For instance, a companion might remark mockingly about the public authority's reaction to a social issue, an assessment we disagree with. Partaking in these discussions can prompt genuine contentions or belittle others. Throughout the long term, I express my feeling, which regularly fills a warmed discussion. I figured out how to tune in and maintain my points of view. I remind myself: "In the event that you can remain silent positive, say nothing."

Participate for the sake of entertainment and significant work or recreation exercises. Probably the most ideal way to manage affliction is to commit our time and energy to what we appreciate. For some, a vocation provides them importance and motivation and fulfillment, while others appreciate relaxation exercises. I understood that composition and photography would give me "Delight de Vivre".

Partaking in human expression. We can forestall cynicism by immunizing anything with fun music, fun workmanship, silly films, astonishing photography, verse composing, wonderful creative mind, imagination. The best verse, journals, and short dreams end with a revelation about the human condition - they share an illustration about existence. I regularly read significant articles, magazines and books, whatever supports my spirit and fills my psyche with good contemplations and sentiments and stories. I additionally appreciate making great motion pictures in the films. This previous summer was an energetic, paramount film Childhood, an anecdote about little youngsters going into youthfulness.

Remembering our good fortune. This straightforward exercise assists us with zeroing in on the up-sides of life. Consistently, we can address the inquiry: What am I appreciative for? Work, love, family, reserve funds are normal reactions. The vast majority don't consider it until they lose their wellbeing. Whenever, mishap, sickness, illness, disaster can completely change us. I know two individuals who are destructive with malignant growth are biting the dust. Since there may not be an opportunity later on, doing is significant now, I have decided to zero in on the present. Assuming it is negative, I will disregard it. Sooner or later in the day, I say thanks to myself for my great wellbeing. I have discovered that in the event that you don't have your wellbeing, your personal satisfaction will be low.

CHAPTER FIFTEEN

Friendship

A few kinships are attractive and wonderful and work on our personal satisfaction. Different kinships bring conflict and difficulty and can be harmful to our wellbeing. Best companionships add significance and reason to our lives, work on our psychological and actual wellbeing, and improve our prosperity.

Studies in Sure Brain science On the off chance that you have at least five companions, they can give social connections and backing in the midst of affliction or stress, you will be more joyful than an individual without companions.

Where do we track down companionships? What are awesome and most exceedingly terrible kinds of kinships? How might we create and keep up with fellowships? How could kinship further develop our prosperity?

Each blend offers the chance for companionship. You have the amazing chance to meet individuals, get to know them and foster companionships in numerous ways. At school; On visit or get-away; Conscious endeavor; Presentation from different companions; In a dance; Mess around; Going to a party; Via web-based media like dating website or Facebook. These companionships are set apart by their motivation, physical allure, connection, closeness,

closeness, worth, interests, etc. We use words like genuine companions, non-romantic companions, normal companions, closest companions, kindred spirits, companions with benefits, friends through correspondence, virtual companions via online media, poisonous fellowships and ex-companions to portray these connections. A few fellowships last some time; Different kinships endure forever.

Kinships self-destruct for various reasons. For instance, when a task companion leaves a task, you lack the opportunity at work to see them. Or then again assuming a companion moves to another city, area, state, or nation - you are more averse to appreciate quality time with them. In some cases kinships end without our own shortcoming. Over the long haul you will separate. At different times either may disregard kinship or gain different kinships. Thus it is truly challenging to keep a companionship.

The best kind of companionship is "dearest companion," trailed by great fellowship. Aristotle said of good companionship: "a similar soul stays in two bodies." Old buddies and great fellowships work on our personal satisfaction. There is holding and association, euphoria and significance, trust and compliance, acclaim. Old buddies and great kinships are difficult to come by and ought to be loved. On the off chance that you have an old buddy for the remainder of your life, you are honored.

What are the attributes of a decent or best companionship? Kinship is attractive, easy going, agreeable, and special somehow or another. For instance, companions are associated with some normal interest like hockey or baseball or theater or craftsmanship.

Companions regard each other by scrutinizing or depreciating or ridiculing one another. Whenever one companion requests counsel, another companion reacts sincerely and consciously.

They invest quality energy with one another. They take part in discussion over espresso, snicker at jokes. They can watch a film, go to a class together, participate in a game, etc. At any rate, companions chat on the phone, keeping distance from investing energy face to face.

Companions trust each other so they can share mysteries realizing that their security won't be disregarded.

Companions are dutiful, consistently steady, particularly when a companion is unfortunate and needs to adapt to difficulty.

They understand the worth of kinship, praise, recall a birthday, send a get-well card, call to say "hi".

Companions praise accomplishments or triumphs. Whenever you succeed, a companion will salute you.

They connect with one another by trading common interests. For instance, assuming you call and communicate something specific, the smart companion will send the get back to. In the event that you welcome them to supper, a smart companion will likewise welcome you to supper. A decent kinship is preposterous without compromising or trade of significant worth.

Indeed, it is smarter to be separated from everyone else and without companions than a harmful individual to your prosperity. A harmed companion will debase your life and toxin your spirit. Perhaps a harmed companion is continually offending you, never praising your victories and having nothing to say. Maybe a harmful companion is continuously grumbling, consistently out of luck and never reacting to one another. Maybe the harmed companion was loudly or truly oppressive or not interested in the fellowship. Perhaps a harmed companion isn't dependably strong, will let you know how to carry on with your life or express desire or jealousy. Maybe the harmed companion is self centered and narcissistic, exploitative, continuously zeroing in on their own requirements and wants. Perhaps the harmful companion has an awful impact, issue with liquor or medications. Perhaps the companion is improper or corrupt.

People are social creatures that need food, cover, clothing, water, as well as affection and social connection. Some of the time this social collaboration is between two darlings, for instance, beau and sweetheart, or companions or joint legitimate accomplices. Kinship is one of the elixirs of a decent life that offers many advantages. Here are some:

Kinship can assist you with adapting to misfortune like employment cutback, ailment, and demise of a companion. Cover a genuine companion in the difficult situation. For instance, when you part ways with a beau or sweetheart, your companions will be close by, offering help and consolation. Closest companions will uphold you in the most exceedingly awful of times.

Great companionship makes a social bond or association somebody imparts exercises and encounters to them. This agreement of kinship makes importance and reason in your life.

Beneficial fellowship brings happiness to your life. For instance, you can sit together in a ball game, snicker at a joke, or participate in discussion. Along with a companion, you can commend a happy time, like winning the Blue Jays Worldwide championship. Regularly, our beloved recollections are of investing energy with companions, maybe going kayaking and setting up camp, climbing bluffs or skiing inclines, or going to any intriguing objective.

Fellowship diminishes pressure in your life. At the point when we are restless or vexed, an old buddy pays attention to our predicament and offers consolation and consistent reassurance.

Great kinships support your confidence and certify your self-esteem. For instance, a companion may say, "I truly like your humor." Then, at that point, tell yourself, "I have a fair of humor."

Companions trust each other so they can share mysteries realizing that their security won't be disregarded.

Companions are dutiful, consistently steady, particularly when a companion is unfortunate and needs to adapt to difficulty.

They understand the worth of kinship, praise, recall a birthday, send a get-well card, call to say "hi".

Companions praise accomplishments or triumphs. Whenever you succeed, a companion will salute you.

They connect with one another by trading common interests. For instance, assuming you call and communicate something specific, the smart companion will send the get back to. In the event that you welcome them to supper, a smart companion will likewise welcome you to supper. A decent kinship is preposterous without compromising or trade of significant worth.

Indeed, it is smarter to be separated from everyone else and without companions than a harmful individual to your prosperity. A harmed companion will debase your life and toxin your spirit. Perhaps a harmed companion is continually offending you, never praising your victories and having nothing to say. Maybe a harmful companion is continuously grumbling, consistently out of luck and never reacting to one another. Maybe the harmed companion was loudly or truly oppressive or not interested in the fellowship. Perhaps a harmed companion isn't dependably strong, will let you know how to carry on with your life or express desire or jealousy. Maybe the harmed companion is self centered and narcissistic, exploitative, continuously zeroing in on their own requirements and wants. Perhaps the harmful companion has an awful impact, issue with liquor or medications. Perhaps the companion is improper or corrupt.

People are social creatures that need food, cover, clothing, water, as well as affection and social connection. Some of the time this social collaboration is between two darlings, for instance, beau and sweetheart, or companions or joint legitimate accomplices. Kinship is one of the elixirs of a decent life that offers many advantages. Here are some:

Kinship can assist you with adapting to misfortune like employment cutback, ailment, and demise of a companion. Cover a genuine companion in the difficult situation. For instance, when you part ways with a beau or sweetheart, your companions will be close by, offering help and consolation. Closest companions will uphold you in the most exceedingly awful of times.

Great companionship makes a social bond or association somebody imparts exercises and encounters to them. This agreement of kinship makes importance and reason in your life.

Beneficial fellowship brings happiness to your life. For instance, you can sit together in a ball game, snicker at a joke, or participate in discussion. Along with a companion, you can commend a happy time, like winning the Blue Jays Worldwide championship. Regularly, our beloved recollections are of investing energy with companions, maybe going kayaking and setting up camp, climbing bluffs or skiing inclines, or going to any intriguing objective.

Fellowship diminishes pressure in your life. At the point when we are restless or vexed, an old buddy pays attention to our predicament and offers consolation and consistent reassurance.

Great kinships support your confidence and certify your self-esteem. For instance, a companion may say, "I truly like your humor." Then, at that point, tell yourself, "I have a fair of humor."

Great fellowships can grow your inclinations and encounters. For instance, a companion might acquaint you with new dishes, books, expressions, film, music, travel, dance.

The people who have an organization of good fellowships can live longer than the individuals who don't.

An old buddy will likewise give you a new viewpoint. You see life according to your own viewpoint and they regularly share an alternate assessment.

Fellowship upgrades our joy and prosperity. They add importance and reason to life.

Last thoughts Blind Helen Keller once said, "I like to stroll with a companion in obscurity rather than alone in the light." Without fellowship, the vast majority live miserable, discouraged and forlorn lives, disengaged and desolate, zeroing in just on themselves and their disappointment. Great companionships require ordinary social connection and shared love. It additionally relies upon regard, social help, trust, compassion and empathy. Great fellowships give joy and delight. Rather than getting things done all alone, we can share normal interests and exercises, as well as offer an excursion through existence with an associate. Great kinships additionally add significance and reason to our lives, significantly working on our emotional well-being and prosperity. The antiquated Greek rationalist Epicurus said: "Of the relative multitude of things that give intelligence to one to live cheerfully ever later, fellowship is the best."

CHAPTER SIXTEEN

Oneself

To live just, we should settle on a cognizant decision to embrace "deliberate straightforwardness." above all, we have the opportunity to pick how to make our lives simpler. We want to consider specific things, for example, further developing balance between fun and serious activities, taking on a superior life, living astutely, partaking in the occasion, investing quality energy and dialing back. Anything that we pick, choices will further develop our prosperity and true serenity.

For what reason would it be advisable for us to think about a basic life? We carry on with a quiet life and a daily existence liberated from turmoil, necessities and intricacy. We delayed down and quit carrying on with a turbulent life, an unpleasant way of life. We figure out how to unwind with private time and isolation. We carry on with a decent existence of euphoria, stream, importance and reason. Regardless of whether everything in life is momentary and everything transforms, we will concentrate our time, energy and monetary assets on what is significant and not hang tight for the emergency. We wipe out disarray, which occupies us from the significant things throughout everyday life. We will actually want to live inside our means and stay away from the weight of obligation. We live shrewdly right now and don't stress over the future or lament the past. We carry on with a healthy lifestyle there will be the ideal opportunity for work, love, family, recreation exercises, wellness and otherworldliness. We have independence from those conditions, responsibilities, obligations and individuals who keep us from carrying on with a decent life. We have the opportunity to live what we need - truly.

How might we improve on our lives? For effortlessness we really want to make a balance between fun and serious activities. We ought to invest energy for work, time for family, an ideal opportunity for sweetheart, time for companions, time for recreation exercises and time for otherworldliness. Studies in certain brain research have shown us how to further develop our prosperity. We should go in three ways: First, we should have a few delight in our life, like going on an outing, engaging in sexual relations or hitting the dance floor with an alluring lady. Zero in on getting the "Gluttonous Treadmill". Bliss is temporary, so we really want to track down seriously enduring satisfaction.

We should figure out how to carry on with an "drew throughout everyday life" by working in a pleasurable and compensating position, by enjoying recreation exercises that give a feeling of stream, by creating significant fellowships, and by investing quality energy with a sweetheart. What is essential to us.

At long last, balance between fun and serious activities needs to add importance and reason to our lives. Intentionally, we can do this by developing our otherworldliness and accepting religion. We want to track down importance past our own conventional lives. It's tied in with defeating "oneself".

We can make our lives more straightforward by surrendering performing multiple tasks. Performing multiple tasks is intricate and debilitates our usefulness. Performing multiple tasks extends our concentration and causes pressure. Prior to setting out on the subsequent undertaking, we can zero in on doing the primary responsibility. All things considered, we should make it a propensity to perform each assignment in turn. We work on our usefulness by finishing each job in turn. For instance, read a book in a tranquil spot without being occupied by TV and phone. By wrapping up each job in turn, you make your life less confounded, on the grounds that you want to concentrate your time and consideration just on one assignment and not a few or four. Performing various tasks resembles six distinct individuals providing you arranges immediately.

We can make our lives more straightforward by disengaging advanced contraptions, including cell phones, tablets and the Web. Advanced innovations are complicated to utilize and expect you to concentrate, which is regularly diverting. While driving, don't message on a cell phone. As you stroll down the road, notice the world with your faculties without talking or messaging on your cell phone. Whenever you are at home, disengage from the convenient music player. While sitting in front of the TV, switch off the tablet. At the point when you converse with a companion, don't get it when your cell phone rings. In the evening, after work, switch off the cell phone and unwind. In contrast to the all day, every day module, invest some private energy unobtrusively and discreetly.

By dialing back we can live just. This implies we want to carve out opportunity to unwind. We can spend an hour daily alone. We can peruse, stand by listening to music, ruminate. We can begin a straightforward work out regime like planning a power walk or doing yoga consistently. We might observe business that doesn't expect us to work extended periods on non-weekend days and ends of the week. We can invest energy sitting idle - and simply thinking or recollecting. Rather than continuously getting it done, we can just decide to "remain".

There are two significant components of information that are important for my way of thinking of living just. The first is to live with some restraint. All in all, I stay away from limits. You won't see me ascending the mountain or dropping from the plane. You won't see me swimming alone in the lake or betting to save my life. I understood that assuming I drank a lot of I would get a headache. Assuming I smoke, I'm in danger for cellular breakdown in the lungs or emphysema. Assuming I fill my plate with low quality nourishment and become accustomed to it, I'm overweight and in danger of medical issues. Assuming that I speed on the expressway, the possibilities of a cop halting and giving me a speeding ticket increment. I understood that making the outrageous excursion would expand my danger of emergency. Emergency entangles life. Emergency regularly prompts difficulty.

Nobody will constrain us to improve on our lives. Living basically is an individual decision. The vast majority see that their lives become not so much upsetting but rather more unsurprising as a component of their life theory. Many likewise observe that life turns out to be less muddled. There are less interruptions, less obligations, less weights, less responsibilities - they drag out our time, exhaust our energy, redirect our consideration from significance and reason, to what exactly is significant for carrying on with a cheerful life. I have discovered that living admirably further develops prosperity, joy and life fulfillment.

CHAPTER SEVENTEEN

GOD

Is there a God? Many people believe in a God who is the "Supreme Being." This God is omniscient, all-powerful, and eternal. Many people believe in God as the "Great Creator" of humanity and the universe. Many people believe in a God who speaks to man's conscience, guiding moral decisions and forgiving sin and other sins. Many people believe in a God who is like a personal friend, who listens to our concerns, anxieties, and tragedies, provides us guidance in tough times, and answers our prayers. Many people believe in a God who intervenes in human events, works miracles, and fulfils predictions.

He can sense that evil lurks in certain men's hearts and brains. I just read of a stranger being stabbed to death on the street for a pack of smokes. Another stalked and kicked and punched a crippled guy to death in a dark park. If you read a little history, you will see how mankind express their fury, hatred, and disdain. Dictators eliminate their enemies through torture, annihilation, and genocide.

There are several religions, each claiming to have discovered the truth. Every religion has its own moral code, and each religion claims to know the way to enlightenment or eternal life. How can we know which religion is right when there are so many? Can everyone be correct?

I am an agnostic, not an atheist. If God exists, I think that his great might is beyond our comprehension. We can't explain God correctly since we've never seen him. As a result, any description is only speculative thought. I believe in the idea of God, but not in a personal God, a superior entity that answers my prayers and leads my life. No God has ever answered my prayers, given me advise, or given me direction.

One of my major questions regarding God is related to pain. Looking around, you can see that much of mankind is suffering. If God is all-powerful and all-knowing, why does he allow so much unfathomable anguish and suffering? Perhaps God endowed humanity with free will. Perhaps God will teach us to be compassionate via our sorrow. I'm not certain. The other question I have concerns evil. Evil, in my opinion, lurks in certain men's hearts and brains. Why would an all-powerful and loving God create bad humans? The response about free will does not entirely answer my question.

I am a skeptic who demands proof, thus my skepticism stops me from promoting a specific faith or stating unequivocally that God exists. The existence of God is a mystery. Nobody knows for certain if God exists. Atheists are unable to demonstrate beyond a reasonable doubt that God does not exist. Religions cannot establish beyond a reasonable doubt that God exists, thus they must rely on trust. As a result, I remain an agnostic, a person who is unsure. In other words, I have no way of knowing whether or not God exists.

And yet, when I consider the order and intricacy of the universe and humans, I am inclined to believe that an ultimate entity exists within the world that is beyond my comprehension. But I don't have definitive proof. As a result, I continue to be a wishful thinker who is suspicious.

My debut book, EMBLEM: POETRY AND PROSE, received a five-star rating on Amazon. Notion Press is the publisher. If you are interested in poetry or prose, you may purchase a book from Amazon, Flipkart, or the Notion Press Store. If you want to keep up with my content and book updates, follow me on Instagram at _selbstuberwindung_

9 798885 914376

Printed by Libri Plureos GmbH in Hamburg,
Germany